What Happened to the American Dream?

By Robert L. Hamlett

© 2012 Robert L. Hamlett
All Rights Reserved.

No part of this publication may be reproduced, stored in a retrieval system, or transmitted, in any form or by any means, electronic, mechanical, photocopying, recording, or otherwise, without the written permission of the author.

First published by Dog Ear Publishing
4010 W. 86th Street, Ste H
Indianapolis, IN 46268
www.dogearpublishing.net

dog ear
PUBLISHING

ISBN: 978-1-4575-1198-1

This book is printed on acid-free paper.

Printed in the United States of America

"Sometimes I wonder whether the world is being run by smart people who are putting us on or by imbeciles who really mean it"

—Mark Twain

CONTENTS

Introduction 1

Chapter 1——-Poverty 3

Chapter 2——-Fat Cats 8

Chapter 3——-Maligned Workers 13

Chapter 4——-National Debt 18

Chapter 5——-Health Care 23

Chapter 6——-Social Security 27

Chapter 7——-Civil Liberties 30

Chapter 8——-Discrimination 34

Chapter 9——-Education 39

Chapter 10——Foreign Policy 46

Chapter 11——Military 50

Chapter 12——Crime 55

Chapter 13——2012 Election 59

INTRODUCTION

After the devastating depression in the 30's and the almost endless World War II in the 40's, which threatened our very existence, the American Dream was reborn. Optimism prevailed that this was indeed a new day for America. Returning soldiers found an America full of wondrous opportunity. Aided by the GI Bill, education was available to millions who might otherwise have been left behind. Opportunities for the average worker seemed endless. Inexpensive housing was readily available to those who worked hard. This fantasy world continued for decades as America reached and maintained a predominate place in the world.

What happened to the American Dream? Today it is but a fantasy of days gone by. Wages for the average "Joe" have declined dramatically as the wealthy and the CEO's of our largest corporations line their pockets with ill-gotten gains! Health care is either unavailable or is beyond the means of millions of our citizens. Pensions to provide a decent life for retired Americans have all but disappeared. Decent housing is beyond the reach of the average citizen. Many of the formerly Middle Class find themselves in desperate straights, struggling to just survive in what appears to be a hostile world. The poor get poorer, the rich get richer and the Middle Class gradually becomes extinct!

This book will delineate the various areas which have transformed our society from one of vast hope to one of survival and why the American Dream is but a faint memory. Is this plight upon our citizens inevitable and destined to continue? The future of Americans depends upon a revival of the indomitable spirit and resolve once displayed by previous generations of Americans. The last chapter of this book will set forth the hard decisions and actions that must take place by all of our citizens to see that the American Dream is restored!

CHAPTER 1

Poverty

THE AMERICAN DREAM has been the fabric of our society since the founding fathers had the courage to declare our independence from Great Britain. It manifested itself in the heartfelt belief that everyone in our society could achieve their dreams through perseverance and hard work. Even in the dark days of the great depression in the 1930's, hope sprang eternal that better days lie ahead and that the American Dream remained a part of our country's destiny.

Today, faith in the American Dream is but a feint memory for many of our citizens. Many Americans have come to realize that America may well have reached its zenith in the late 1900's and that for most Americans a decline in their standard of living is all but inevitable.

Today's young people, even those fortunate enough to have a degree from a college or university, will find decent jobs hard to come by. This is very disconcerting to these young people since they realize that often college graduates of previous generations had multiple offers of employment. Most of the young had assumed that a college degree was a ticket to the "good life". Instead, many are forced to accept the only job offer they receive, even if it is far below their expectations. Some graduates can find no employer willing to give them a chance and face the prospect of long-term unemployment.

This is but the tip of the iceberg! Many college graduates, especially those from low or modest income families, face tremendous liabilities for massive student loans that they must repay. With jobs far below those that they had expected, they find it is necessary to "pay the piper", even though their meager resources many times force them to live lives barely above the poverty line. Incredibly, the total amount of outstanding student loans, which must be repaid by those barely existing, exceeds the total amount of credit card debt of all of our citizens! This is in spite of the fact that Americans have been on a "buying frenzy" for some time, charging on credit cards far more than they can afford. Ultimately, many young people will be forced to default on their student loans, imperiling their credit rating and facing a dismal future.

Even young people fortunate enough to find good jobs will find that liberal fringe benefits, once routinely furnished employees, have been slashed to the bone. Medical benefits, one of the prime reasons people seek full-time jobs, now have deductibles and co-pays requiring an employee to spend a great deal more out-of-pocket should he or she require medical treatment. Those young people with an ingrained work ethic often are forced to seek temporary employment just to survive. Most "Temp" jobs provide meager wages and absolutely no fringe benefits. Even worse, there is absolutely no job security! "Temps" may be fired at the whim of an employer, without cause or justification!

Unfortunately, in America poverty is now the norm rather than an aberration. Once, the underclass of society consisted primarily of helpless and hopeless "welfare mothers", who were the subject of ridicule and disdain. Today, even many of those with full-time employment find themselves in desperate straights and have joined the ranks of the impoverished. In addition, poverty, once confined to the inner city, has now spread to the once affluent suburbs. Many previously middle class citizens living in the suburbs are perplexed and dismayed they often share the lot with the inner city poor.

As the middle class spirals downward, fifty million people find themselves in the ranks of the impoverished. Not unexpectedly, children are many times the innocent victims of this disastrous decline in the lives of Americans. Over one and one-half million young people are now living hopeless lives, either homeless or are living "on the streets", at the mercy of the baser elements in our society.

As might be expected, the result of this increase in poverty and desperation rampant in America is an increase in crime. Of course, the wealthy, living in gated communities, among other affluent citizens, are "fat, dumb and happy", impervious to the crime suffered by ordinary Americans.

As for average Americans, they must be constantly vigilant, less a desperate person come to believe that committing a crime against innocent citizens is their "only salvation"! Even otherwise moral people, when pushed far enough, are capable of unspeakable acts. As delineated in Bob Dylan's song "Like a Rolling Stone":

> "When you ain't got nothing,
> You got nothing to lose"

How did America, once the land of plenty, fall into such an era of such desperate plight? In the past twenty years, ninety percent of American workers saw their wages rise a paltry 15 percent. Did all Americans share equally in this stagnant economy? Hardly! The 400 wealthiest Americans saw incomes increase an average of 400 percent! At the very least, did not our country benefit from taxes on these richest of the rich?

Guess again! During this period, the nation's wealthiest households paid, on average, the lowest taxes in history!

Could not the federal government have intervened to prevent this disintegration of American society? The government did act during the eight year presidency of George W. Bush. His actions did, in fact, have a huge impact on the direction of our country. Unfortunately for our society and the future of the country, his actions greatly acerbated the huge income gap between the average working man and the wealthy among us!

Irresponsibly, President Bush commenced two completely unwarranted and unnecessary wars, first in Iraq, then in Afghanistan. The war in Iraq lasted nine years before President Obama had the good sense to bring our troops home and leave the Iraqis to determine their own fate. The war in Afghanistan has lasted ten years with no end in sight. The best Americans can hope for is an eventual negotiated settlement, while attempting to save a little "face". These two irresponsible wars have cost American tax payers will over a trillion dollars; cost thousands of lives of our brave fighting men, with thousands more suffering horrendous injuries.

The above blunders are a major reason that our country's national debt has escalated to the point where it threatens America's economic future. Not content with putting the country's future in peril by useless wars, President Bush continued the treachery, with the help of a Republican Congress, by passing massive tax cuts to benefit America's wealthiest citizens. Further, to ensure that his rich cronies had the best of all worlds, President Bush, with help from his Republican cohorts in crime in Congress, passed legislation eliminating previous barriers from outsourcing good American jobs to third world countries, where labor could be obtained for a pittance.

In 2009, when President Obama, a Democrat, assumed office, the country could hardly have been in worse shape economically. There were no satisfactory options for the new president. He had to choose between attempting to reduce the out-of-control national debt and letting our citizens suffering escalate with probable needless deaths, or attempting to minimize the suffering by humanitarian and compassionate assistance from the government. To his credit, he chose the latter.

The U.S. House of Representatives, controlled by reactionary Republicans and their partners in crime, the mindless Tea Party, has no concern for suffering Americans. Their mindset is the same as the French monarch over two hundred years ago with regard to suffering citizens:

"Let them eat cake"

CHAPTER 2

Fat Cats

AMERICANS HAVE ALWAYS assumed that the way to a better life is to work hard and persevere in pursuit of their dreams. Unfortunately, as illustrated in the chapter on poverty, most Americans now have little chance of obtaining the American Dream. Poverty breeds poverty, with each generation of the underclass following in the footsteps of those that went before them, with little hope that their lot in life will ever improve.

What is the secret of living the "good life", as promised by the American Dream? The easiest path to live in the lap of luxury is to inherit massive assets from wealthy parents or other relatives. This does not require the recipient of this bounty to contribute "one wit" to society or in any way to help improve the lot of those less fortunate.

In the past, an estate tax, although woefully inadequate, at least provided a semblance of the deceased's wealth partially going to the benefit of society and their fellow countrymen. That small contribution is quickly fading away. Today, the estate tax is the lowest in nearly a century. With Republicans and their mindless Tea Party fellow travelers now firmly in control of the House of Representatives, and the possibility of a reactionary Republican occupying the White house in 2013, it would not be surprising to see the estate tax be relegated to a thing of the past.

Already, the elitist Republicans have managed to reduce the tax on long-term capital gains from 40% to a paltry 15% today. The Republican's goal is to completely eliminate the tax on long-term capital gains. Of course, since almost all of stocks held by our citizens are in the hands of the rich, with the average American content to just scrape by and pay their current bills, elimination of this tax will only go to enhance the coffers of the wealthy and further increase the disparity in wealth between the rich and hard working, but poor, Americans.

So, does the average working man have any chance of his seeing the American Dream fulfilled? Hardly! As noted before, millions upon millions of our countrymen are mired in poverty, without hope of ever seeing improvement in their lot. Even those fortunate to have what they consider "good" jobs actually have far less purchasing power than any time within memory. Not surprisingly, the 10% of our country's wealthiest citizens now own 50% of the nation's total wealth! The disparity between the "haves" and the "have-not's" is the greatest since the founding of our great country.

Surprisingly, Republicans have been successful in convincing otherwise intelligent Americans that their agenda is not only best for individuals but also best for the country. They have sold Americans a "bill of goods" that lower taxes on both the wealthy and rich corporations is in the best interest of our economy and each individual citizen.

Lower taxes on both the wealthy and hugely profitable corporations produce two disastrous results. First, it greatly increases an already out-of-control National Debt, which imperils America's economic well-being. Secondly, with no funds available to mend our country's long-ignored infrastructure, the condition of America's schools, roads, interstates, and other physical assets will deteriorate with a resultant deep decline in our standard of living. Apparently, the electorate is oblivious to this impending calamity.

Republicans also bemoan the prospects of America's "suffering" corporations. However, they ignore the fact that the after-tax profits, for these "beleaguered" corporations, are the highest in our nation's history. Republicans point, with dismay, at the "theoretical" tax rate for corporations, saying it is unfair and stifles competition with overseas companies. In reality, the effective tax rate for such corporations is actually only 15%. However, never underestimate the ability of American corporate bosses to avoid legal taxes and inflate the earnings of their corporations.

Of our country's leading profitable corporations, over 10%, through manipulating the tax code to their advantage, actually pay no taxes at all! Many actually get refunds! Disgustingly, for the unfortunate U. S. corporations that actually did pay taxes, several actually spent more lobbying Congress than they paid in taxes. How do they manage such "Shenanigans"? Some merely shift many of their operating units overseas. Others find and exploit loopholes in our own massive confusing tax code to their advantage.

Republicans also point to the "enormous" taxes paid by corporate America as the reason these corporations refuse to hire American workers. Naturally, the lack of jobs results in an unacceptably high unemployment rate. If taxation is or was the problem, why did President George W. Bush's massive tax cuts during his presidency not result in any significant hiring by the corporate world? These greedy corporations, with no loyalty to America's workers or to the country that bestowed upon them great opportunity, have a hidden agenda to ensure that corporate profits go "through the roof". They merely ship American jobs overseas, where they can obtain workers at a pittance of what they would have to pay American workers.

Almost one and one-half million American jobs are now in the hands of third world workers.

Have the Chief Executive Officers of our nation's giant corporations suffered during our economic downturn to the same extent as their employees and the average citizen? Not on your life! Even when corporations are honest and actually pay taxes due, a great many CEO's are being paid more than their corporations pay in taxes! In addition, the heads of our nation's corporations ensure that they themselves will never suffer the same fate as their employees. When things go badly for a corporation, the CEO's "bail out", taking with them the proceeds of their "golden parachutes", huge paydays, often exceeding 100 million dollars.

Republicans are obsessed with the deregulation of the corporate world. This is not surprising since they receive enormous campaign contributions from their wealthy corporate benefactors. Ever since the U.S. Supreme Court, dominated by Republican presidential appointees, held that corporations are "people" and, thus, there is no limit to the amount they can contribute to their Republican political "servants", competition between the political parties has been "one-sided". Since Democrats have no equivalent "sugar daddy", it is hard for Democrats to be competitive in political contests for our nation's Congressional seats. Not surprisingly, Republicans have been successful in removing effective regulation of Wall Street and the other financial institutions. As a result, during the last few months of President George W. Bush's reign, the financial community began unraveling at an alarming rate. A complete collapse was barely averted.

Although it is hard to fathom why the average voter has not turned against the Republican Party for overreaching, the Republicans have unabashedly successfully promoted that the country should go to a "flat tax", instead of a tax code that "theoretically" resulted in the tax rate increasing the more income one made. This would result in a person making the minimum wage having the same tax rate as a billionaire! Even one of America's richest men, to his credit, agreed that the wealthy were not paying their fair share of taxes.

The founding fathers envisioned a land of equal opportunity for all. They must be turning over in their graves seeing the country they founded being a haven only for the rich, with the average American doomed to a life of mere survival.

CHAPTER 3

Maligned workers

SINCE THE TIME of the founding fathers, it has been basic to the American Dream that every generation live better than those that came before them. In spite of the "blip" on America's screen during the great depression of the 30's, Americans that came of age during World War II or thereafter led the "good life" as anticipated. Due to the massive technological advances during that period, all but the very poorest among us led very comfortable lives.

Enthusiasm reigned supreme as nothing seemed beyond America's reach. Separated from the rest of the world by two vast oceans, American workers, many of whom belonged to unions, competed only with other Americans for good paying jobs. The days when American workers were forced to compete with cheap labor in the underdeveloped world were far in the future.

Most families fared well with only one spouse holding down a job. Most worked only a five day work-week, eight hours a day, and had paid vacations. Pensions for workers, to sustain them when they reached the age of retirement, were available to a great many in the work force. American workers were leading "the life of Riley"!

American workers were the envy of laborers throughout the world. Shortly after President John F. Kennedy took office in 1961, he promised that by the end of the decade, America would put a man on the surface of the moon. In July 1969, although President Kennedy was longer with us, the promise was fulfilled.

A primary reason for the optimism of our citizens dated back to the administration of Franklin Roosevelt in the 30's, when he initiated a "New Deal" for Americans, innovative and compassionate policies which were long overdue. At that time, our country and its citizens faced a desperate plight due to the failed policies of Republican President Herbert Hoover.

When did the American workers life begin to unravel? As best that can be determined, things began to go downhill for American workers approximately thirty years ago. Not coincidentally, 1980 was the year that our citizens elected a conservative Republican zealot, Ronald Reagan, to the office of the presidency. Although he had promised a shining light on the hill, the lights began a steady dim for American workers.

Greatly magnifying the problem for our workers, during the eight year reign of George W. Bush which began in 2001, was the astronomical increase in the disparity in wealth between the rich and the average worker. While corporate profits soared, along with the compensation to corporations' executives, millions of Americans either became unemployed or vastly under-employed. Without concern for America's workers, good jobs were shipped overseas by nihilistic corporate executives whose only concern was enhancing ever-increasing corporate profits. Millions of American workers lucky enough to obtain employment often worked for a "pittance" at manual jobs far below their abilities. Today, the average compensation for America's workers has fallen to 27,000 dollars a year! America's Middle Class is disappearing at an alarming rate.

American consumers are partly to blame for the plight of the American worker. They flock to stores selling goods made overseas by foreign workers who will work for little or nothing. Even though American made goods may be superior in quality, the price differential between American made products and those produced overseas is sufficient to lure American consumers. As a result, with the exception of military hardware necessary to defend our country, very little is now actually produced in America. Manufacturing jobs are increasingly obsolete in most American industries. We have now become a nation where most workers are employed in jobs providing "services" to other citizens rather than producing anything of value.

Another aspect of American life contributing to the "downfall" of the average American worker is the highly technical nature of the dwindling number of jobs available in this country. Many workers whose skills were satisfactory in the past find that they are no longer technologically qualified to fill today's employment needs. Young people usually are more up-to-date on today's technology and are hired for jobs that older workers are unable to perform. But things are not "rosy" for young workers. There are so few highly technical jobs available and a multitude of young people without work, that the competition for these jobs is enormous. Consequently, these young workers, desperate for work, are forced to accept meager wages just to survive. As for the technology-challenged older workers, too young to be eligible for Social Security benefits, a great many go back to educational facilities to either upgrade their skills in their prior field or to seek training in a completely different field where workers are now desperately needed.

Today's employees are fortunate indeed if they receive good "fringe benefits" in connection with their employment. In many cases, employment carries with it negligible fringe benefits compared with employees of yesteryear. The most important benefit to most employees is health care assistance provided by the employer. Some older workers put off retirement and stay employed more for the health care coverage than the meager wages they receive. Even so, employers are tending to require employees to shoulder a much greater share of health care costs.

Even though the plight of those lucky enough to obtain a full-time job is declining, those desperate enough to obtain work as temporary workers have it even worse. "Temps" have absolutely no job security. They can be fired at the whim of the employer. In addition, their wages, which are most often meager, are their only compensation. They have absolutely no fringe benefits! The American Dream has become but a "cruel joke" to most of our citizens. Not only are they forced to work for "peanuts", there is little prospect that their lives will improve anytime soon.

The irony of the above situation is that many of those suffering most ardently support Republican candidates for public office. Lost upon these "disillusioned voters", responsive to Republican dogma, is the fact that policies of the Republican Party are largely responsible for the concentration of the nation's wealth in the favored few at the expense of not only America's workers but our society as a whole.

A major tactic in the Republicans' objective to enrich the wealthy at the expense of the Middle Class is to destroy organized labor. The advent of organized labor unions was a major reason the lives of the average worker vastly improved from the conditions prevalent during the "Dark Days" of the early twentieth century until the present time. Today, Unions are under attack as never before. Over 30,000 workers have been fired attempting to form unions in their companies! Another tactic used by Republicans and their wealthy benefactors is in the enactment of innocent sounding "Right to Work" legislation in as many states as possible. The Southern states are particularly "ripe" for this union bashing tactic; however, recently this tactic has even been successful in a "rust belt" state. Presently, 23 states, primarily where Republicans control politically, have adopted these laws.

Right to Work laws not only affect members of organized labor but all workers in the jurisdiction in which they are in effect. Wages for all workers are much lower in states where collective bargaining is not permitted. The worse aspect of destroying organized labor is the vulnerability of the individual worker. In numbers there is strength! Where there are unions, a worker is not subject to arbitrary dismissal or otherwise mistreatment at the whim of the employer. Where organized labor does not exist, each individual has no recourse for any transgression against him or her.

How do Republicans gain control of state governments? It's simple. In politics, money is the "gorilla" in the room! Corporate America and the wealthy among us pour unlimited resources to elect Republicans to political office, where naturally, they will do their bidding. Right to Work legislation is at the top of the list of priorities of both the Republicans and their wealthy benefactors. What happens once a state becomes a "Right to Work State"? Not surprisingly, the corporations move their operations to such states, where workers receive only minuscule wages while the wealthy become even wealthier! Disdain for the American worker knows no bounds among the rich and their Republican "lapdogs".

Will the "put upon" average working man and woman ever come to their senses and realize that by supporting Republicans for political office they help elect those whose every act is contrary to their own best interests? If they don't "wise up" in time for the 2012 presidential and Congressional elections, it may be too late!

CHAPTER 4

National Debt

AN EXTREMELY IMPORTANT problem in America that greatly affects the standard of living of all our citizens is the ever-expanding uncontrollable national debt. The skyrocketing debt has not only placed a tremendous burden on the budget of all federal programs designed to benefit our citizens and protect them from the ravages of downturns in the economy but has greatly affected state government programs, many dependent on federal funds as well. At present time, no steps are being taken to address our aging and deteriorating infrastructure and, most importantly, funds for the education of our youth is in serious decline. Many states with underfunded budgets have made important educational programs the primary target for reduction or elimination!

What are the factors resulting in such dire circumstances? The out-of-control national debt first reared its ugly head during the presidency of Republican Ronald Reagan, worshipped by present day Republicans. Although unrecognized by our citizenry, during President Reagan's eight year reign, the national debt increased by an astonishing 189 percent! Nothing was done to address the problem during the four year presidency of "do nothing" president, the first George Bush.

When President Bill Clinton assumed the presidency following President Bush, he faced not only an escalating national debt but a "basketful" of other problems. Problematically, while attempting to address the inherited issues, for a large part of his eight year presidency, he faced a Congress dominated by extremely conservative Republicans who fought him "tooth and nail". Despite the almost unanimous opposition of the Republican Congress, in 2001, when he turned over the reins of government to Republican George W. Bush, President Clinton left behind a legacy of prosperity. He had achieved what had seemed impossible, completely eliminating the enormous national debt and leaving the new president with a large budget surplus!

It did not take long for things to unravel! Through no fault of his own, a few months after President Bush assumed office, the nation suffered a horrific destructive "sneak attack" on September 11, 2001. Every American was outraged at the tremendous loss of life and limb on "9-11" and the audacity of any enemy to "thumb its nose" at America and its democratic institutions. Subsequently, a nation bent on "payback" appeared to give President Bush a "blank check" to retaliate. Ordaining President Bush with such unlimited power later proved to be an enormous mistake!

When it became apparent that most of the extremist perpetrators of "9-11" had come from Afghanistan, it was a rational decision by President Bush to seek out and destroy the enemies of America in Afghanistan. An "all-out" short-lived military strike against these enemies of America would have been reasonable and appropriate action. However, consumed with power, President Bush attempted the impossible, "a fool's errand" the formation of a democratic government in Afghanistan. What could have been a relatively inexpensive military action, with only limited casualties, has turned into a "war without end". As of 2012, the war has reached its tenth anniversary. When the fighting in Afghanistan finally ends, the best that Americans can hope for is a negotiated settlement, leaving Afghanistan much as it was before. In addition to the massive amount wasted on this misadventure, enormously contributing to the out-of-control national debt, the thousands of American casualties will have suffered in vain.

Another decision by President Bush in the first year of his presidency, an unwarranted invasion of Iraq, not only led to the overextension of our military, precluding an "all-out" attack on the "9-11" perpetrators in Afghanistan, but commenced yet another endless war. Even worse, this military action was detrimental to the delicate balance of power which had existed in the Middle East. Not long after the invasion began, President Bush brazenly declared "victory" in Iraq, ignorant of the fact that the war had scarcely began and would last almost ten years. In 2011, President Obama wisely called an end to the war and brought our troops home. Even after ten years of war, the fate of Iraq, with its centuries' old animosity between religious factions, is uncertain. Like Afghanistan, the war in Iraq not only has astronomically increased our nation's national debt, but has also resulted in death and debilitating injuries to thousands of our military heroes and has contributed to Americans beginning to question the decisions and values of their government.

As if the two above unnecessary and disastrous wars were not enough to "burst the budget", President Bush's administration, along with a compliant Republican dominated Congress, spent money like proverbial "drunken sailors". Our financial resources were wasted on unnecessary and useless defense and domestic programs and projects neither desired by nor benefiting the average citizen.

As if the above items were not enough to seriously impair America's economic future, incredulously, President Bush and his Republican "lap dogs" in Congress had the audacity to enact tremendous tax cuts for our wealthiest citizens, leaving the

Middle Class to shoulder the burden of the expense of the two wars and the expanding government. Not surprisingly, the "wealth gap" between the rich and the average citizen is now the greatest in our country's history. With the national debt seriously jeopardizing our nation's future, President Bush's "draft dodging" vice-president amazingly has chimed in that "deficits don't matter"! Now the current federal tax rate is the lowest in 60 years. In 2009, when President Bush's eight year disaster was over, the torch was turned over to newly elected President Obama. What a hell of a mess to inherit!

Ever since President Obama assumed office, Congressional Republicans not only criticized his every effort to solve the nation's enormous problems, but had sufficient clout to stymie his every effort to stimulate the economy and correct the wrongs of President George W. Bush's disastrous tenure in office. President Obama's attempts to eliminate the tax cuts for the rich enacted during the Bush years went nowhere. Republicans, despite convincing evidence to the contrary, were adamant in claiming that tax cuts were the best means of creating the demand for workers throughout the country. However, the tax cuts had happened years before. Where were the jobs? Inexplicably, desperate for someone to blame for the morass, many citizens chose to ignore the true culprits, Republicans and their Tea Party cohorts and instead blamed the most visible public official, President Obama. Since President Obama was not up for re-election in 2010, suffering voters took out their frustrations on the nearest target, Congressional Democrats. The Republicans and Tea Party extremists overwhelmingly carried the day in the 2010 mid-term elections, ensuring that any proposal by President Obama to address the country's massive problems had absolutely no chance of being enacted! Their entire focus became on defeating President Obama's bid for re-election in 2012!

Most Americans still are not cognizant of the Republican's and Tea Party's "hidden agenda", that by constantly lowering taxes, to destroy all "New Deal" programs enacted during the

Roosevelt years and the "Great Society" programs of President Lyndon Johnson to provide a "safety net" for the average working man and woman and the less fortunate in our society! Most average Americans are clueless to the fact that should Republicans and Tea Party faithful have their way, Social Security, Medicaid, Medicare and similar programs will soon come but a distant memory.

The only sane approach to addressing the problem of the massive national debt is obvious. First, all present federal programs should have extensive review to eliminate duplication of services and to distinguish between programs which provide essential services and those which can be eliminated or "paired back" without serious detriment to our vulnerable citizens. However, the essential action necessary, which is impossible as long as extremist Republicans and the Tea Party control House of Representatives, is to drastically increase taxes on the wealthy, the only Americans with sufficient funds to incur a tremendous tax increase without changing their life style "one iota"!

CHAPTER 5

Health Care

IN MANY WAYS, America's system of health care is the best in the world, attracting many from around the world to come here to seek treatment or care. However, it is extremely costly. The cost of our health care system amounts to over 17% of our economy, by far the most costly in the world! To address this growing problem, in 2010 President Obama initiated health care reform, better known (derisively) as "ObamaCare". This attempt to address the massive health care problem has incurred the wrath of Republicans everywhere. This program has been challenged in the courts as being unconstitutional by many states, primarily those states where the state government is controlled by Republicans. The fate of "ObamaCare" will ultimately be determined by the decision of U. S. Supreme Court as to its Constitutionality, which most likely, will not occur until late in the spring of 2012, long after this book "goes to press"!

Why the urgency to "do something" about the tremendous cost of health care to our citizens? Even though millions are uninsured, over 20% of other Americans have difficulty paying their medical bills. Insurance policies, written by insurance companies with the companies' best interest in mind, are full of "exclusions", "deductibles" and other ways of limiting liability of the insurer. In addition, premiums for such policies are going "through the roof"!

Even though this new law will not take full effect until 2014, provisions of "ObamaCare" currently in effect have riled the Republicans! Republicans, who are "in bed" with the insurance companies, are "up in arms" over the increased accessibility to health care for people with pre-existing conditions. America's four largest insurance companies in the past had denied coverage to approximately 15% of their policyholders who had pre-existing conditions. Even pregnancy had been considered a pre-existing condition. Republicans and the insurance industry wished to maintain the "status quo".

The new program provided extended coverage for young adults and those with medical issues. Presently, 2.5 million previously uninsured young adults have coverage. It also provided tax credits for some employers to enable them to afford providing employees with health insurance coverage. Among other things, the new program also provided massive funds to establish or improve community health centers, enabled states to expand Medicare coverage for the millions of low-income citizens, enabled Americans to receive preventive care and provided major cost savings for older Americans when purchasing needed prescription drugs.

In addition to the above, by far the most controversial provision of the new law requires most Americans to purchase health care insurance. However, without this provision, the new health care law is unsustainable! The argument against requiring citizens to purchase health care insurance is illogical. Take the example of drivers' licenses, which all states require all persons to have before they can "hit the road". Although those who not drive are not required to have drivers' licenses, **_"every single American will at some time in their life need some form of health care"_**! Today, responsible citizens who purchase health care insurance, in effect, are subsidizing the millions of Americans who do not have such insurance. When the millions of uninsured need and seek medical treatment they receive free medical care. However, it is not really free. Those who provide for their own care by having adequate medical insurance, pay greatly increased premiums to insurance companies to cover the costs of those receiving free health care! It is the provision to require Americans to purchase health care insurance which is the subject of the legal controversy over the Constitutionality of "ObamaCare". Its fate will be ultimately be determined by the decision of the U.S. Supreme Court, where justices appointed by Republican presidents are in the majority.

After the 2010 midterm election, the newly elected U. S. House of Representatives was comprised of a combination of reactionary Republicans and "clueless" members of the Tea Party. Not surprisingly, their first order of business was to attempt to repeal health care reform, "ObamaCare" which had been enacted in the previous session of Congress. Insurance companies and other self-serving lobbyists contributed heavily in the attempt to repeal the act, hoping to turn back the clock to the "good ole days", when they had a stranglehold on health care for Americans. Fortunately for our country, the Democrats still had a 53-47 majority in the U.S. Senate and soundly rejected this proposal. With President Obama having the right to veto in his pocket, obviously, proponents of repeal knew that their efforts would be unproductive. This was merely a "grand-stand" play to mollify extreme elements of both Republicans and the Tea Party and attempt to convert suffering Americans to their cause.

In their livid opposition to "ObamaCare", desperate Republican and Tea Party operatives even drummed up the long discarded issue of "states' rights", claiming that the federal government was "trampling upon the rights of the states". The last time this outdated tactic was used was by segregationists after President Lyndon Johnson and a Democratic Congress passed civil rights legislation relieving black people of carrying the burden of being "second class citizens". To modern day extremists, the more things change, the more they remain the same!

After President Obama assumed the office of the presidency, he realized the necessity for health care reform, observing the obvious fact that health care costs were escalating at an alarming rate and threatened to bankrupt not only a great many Americans but the country as well. Despite some flaws, health care reform was a giant step in the right direction. All elected officials, rather than attempt to destroy the law, should seek ways to improve it. Otherwise, our country will assuredly return to its previous untenable disastrous course. The "chickens will come home to roost" in a few years when millions of aging "baby boomers" require extensive medical care.

CHAPTER 6

Social Security

IN THE 30'S during the Great Depression, many Americans, without work or any means of support, faced a desperate plight. Many were forced to swallow their pride and do everything imaginable, including selling apples on the street corner. Some even chose to take their own lives. After President Franklin Roosevelt's election in 1932, he came to realize that our citizens were in need of a "safety net", to provide sustenance when times were bad. Thus, the Social Security Program, the crown jewel of the president's "New Deal" was born. Since the inception of the Social Security Program, Republicans have continuously attempted to destroy the program.

In 1983, realizing that when the "baby boomers" retired, there would exist a potential crisis looming in the Social Security program, the government began contributing to and building up a Social Security Trust Fund. Eventually, this trust fund amounted to 2.6 trillion dollars. However, down through the years, due to irresponsible fiscal decisions by our leaders to "borrow" from the trust fund to pay for general obligations of the government, this massive trust fund has almost been completely depleted! Sooner or later, the government must "pay the piper" and, once again, build up the trust fund to secure the future of older Americans.

Inexplicably, a primary reason that a great many of our citizens have presently fallen in love with the Republican Party, is their vow to eliminate "waste" in government by cutting or eliminating many entitlement programs and refusing any tax increase, even if such an increase only affected the wealthiest Americans. Many citizens "Buy into" Republican claims that entitlement programs only help the "undeserving". Republicans may very well be successful in winning the 2012 presidential and Congressional elections by "hoodwinking" millions of elderly citizens who depend on Social Security benefits and other entitlement programs. If so, they will eventually come to realize that by abandoning the Democratic Party, they "bit the hand that fed them"!

Buried in the Republican Party's highly publicized "Road Map for America's Future", and not ever mentioned by Republicans seeking public office for fear of alienating elderly voters, is a proposal to "privatize" Social Security! This discredited concept was first proposed by President George W. Bush, during his disastrous eight years in office, but, thankfully, died a quiet death. One current Republican member of Congress from Wisconsin has even proposed that not only Social Security, but Medicare as well, be privatized!

What would have happened to America's senior citizens if during Present George Bush's presidency, his proposal to "privatize" Social Security had actually been passed by Congress and had become the law of the land? The "safety net" of Social Security would no longer have been available to them. Due to the "Stock Market Crash" of 2008, older Americans would have found themselves in desperate straights! With many of their other investments decimated and becoming almost worthless, they would no longer have been able to maintain even a meager existence without the benefit of Social Security income. But what would have become of the wealthiest Americans, backbone of the Republican Party? Surely, they too would have had to withstand diminished income and some loss of wealth: however, they would have continued to lead the "good life", without one thought or concern for the "little people" who suffered so much!

CHAPTER 7

Civil Liberties

THE U. S. CONSTITUTION created by the founding fathers was the defining instrument to protect the new country and its citizens. However, upon further reflection, they realized that the Constitution alone was insufficient to protect the rights and civil liberties of all Americans. Thus, they enacted the "Bill of Rights", codified in the first ten amendments to the Constitution, delineating the basic rights of our citizens. They, most likely, never foresaw that these civil liberties would be the subject of attack throughout our history, even up until the present day.

A major onslaught against the basic rights of Americans began shortly after the terrorist attack on the Twin Towers in New York City and the Pentagon in Washington, D.C. on September 11, 2001, known forever as "9-11". Americans and their elected representatives, who became obsessed with National Security, were determined to take all actions necessary to make the "bastards" pay for their despicable attacks. The civil liberties of Americans were ignored. Unfortunately, in the hysteria following "9-11", Congress stampeded, with little discussion or dissent, to enact the "Patriot Act", supposedly to protect America but which completely ignored the rights and civil liberties of our citizens. President George W. Bush quickly signed this act into law.

In addition to the subsequent reduction of Americans' basic rights following the enactment of the Patriot Act by our federal government, just as ominous to the rights of our countrymen, state governments have recently joined in the attack on our basic freedoms. Within the past two years, Republican in over 30 states have either enacted or in the process of attempting to enact legislation discouraging, or outright denying, certain categories of citizens the basic right to vote for our elected officials. The targets of this purge are poor whites, minorities, college aged young adults, and aged handicapped citizens. What do these groups have in common to be under such vitriolic attack by Republicans? Not surprisingly, members of each of these groups tend to vote overwhelmingly for candidates of the Democratic Party.

The mechanism used to attempt to disenfranchise the millions of citizens noted above is the enactment in states where Republicans are in control, state laws requiring that before anyone can cast their ballot at the polls, they must present a government issued form of identification. The Republicans' supposed justification for this requirement is to prevent "fraud" in the election process. It should be noted that since the "bad ole days" in the 50's and 60's when big city corrupt officials often "stole elections", fraud has not been a significant problem in our country's elections.

The "Picture ID" which will be used by almost all voters will be their state's drivers' license. However, our poorest citizens often do not own an automobile, thus no need for a license to drive. Also, the new laws also make residency requirement more stringent, thus prohibiting many college students, who may be more transient, from voting. In addition, the elderly, many of whom have mobility issues, may be incapable of going to state offices to acquire the required "Picture

ID". The disenfranchisment of millions of our most vulnerable citizens is a " new low" for the Republican party.

When I was a young man in the 60's, many office-holding Republicans were moderates on both national and international issues. Some, like John Lindsay of New York, were outright liberals! Present day Republicans are a different breed! Along with their out-of-touch Tea Party cohorts, Republicans are now extremely reactionary, opposing every item of progressive legislation. Most oppose birth control, stem-cell research, sex education and all abortions, even when the girl is very young and the victim of either rape or incest. Even though Planned Parenthood's primary mission is to provide contraception and health care services, and abortion services are a minor part of their agenda, The Republican and Tea Party dominated U. S. House of Representatives attempted to cut off all funds to Planned Parenthood. Fortunately for women and our country, the Democratic controlled U.S. Senate put an end to such mean-spirited nonsense.

In early 2012, President Obama "took on" the Republican dominated religious right by administratively providing our nation's women access to free birth control. Male leaders of the Catholic Church and fellow-travelers in the Republican Party were outraged, promising retribution in the 2012 presidential election. One Republican politician even went so far as to give his suggestion of an alternative to the "pill", "a woman putting an aspirin between her knees"! Ironically, Republicans failed to note that almost all women have at one time or another used birth control methods, making this an "empty threat". Thus, the hope of Republicans to make President Obama a one-term president may be of no avail as millions of women flock to his cause.

States where Republicans control are continuously "dreaming up" new ways to interfere with the rights of our people. The most extreme example is in Mississippi, both the most religious and reactionary state in the union. The Republican controlled Mississippi government attempted to pass an amendment to the state Constitution which would, in effect, criminalize almost all forms of birth control. This was too much for even for extremely conservative Mississippians, as the attempt to amend the state Constitution was soundly defeated.

Yet another attack on our civil liberties is taking place in states throughout the nation. This time it is a backlash against freedom of speech. More and more complaints are being vehemently expressed by outraged conservative parents over the content of reading material provided their children in public schools. Even advanced placement and college prep courses are under attack. These complainants are primarily members of the religious right, who demand that objectionable material be removed from public schools. They ignore the fact that the purpose of education is to expose students to a broad range of ideas and opinions, so that the students are not locked into a narrow uncompromising view of the world, but are free to explore new concepts in this ever-changing world.

With external threats from terrorists and other yet unknown sources forever emblazoned in the minds of Americans, it is perhaps not surprising that the importance of our citizens' basic rights and civil liberties are sometimes forgotten or ignored. However, to put things in perspective, every American should heed the advice of that patriotic founding father Benjamin Franklin, who once stated:

"They that can give up essential liberty to obtain a little temporary safety deserve neither liberty nor safety."

CHAPTER 8

Discrimination

AMERICA HAS BEEN a shining light in the world for freedom since its inception in the late 1700's following our victory over the British in the Revolutionary War. Of course, that assumed that you were white! Long before the birth of our nation, black people had been brought to America as slaves. The American Revolution did nothing to alter the status of these enslaved black people. In fact, racism was codified in our new Constitution, declaring that, in a census of our country, a black person would only be counted as "Three-fifths of a person"!

A hundred years after a bitter and divisive civil war had divided our country, supposedly, black people could live as free citizens. But that was only in theory. In fact, blacks were forced to live in a segregated society, particularly in the South, suffering the indignity of being second class citizens in their own country. The rights of black citizens, again theoretically, took a great leap forward shortly after Lyndon B. Johnson assumed the office of presidency following the assassination of President Kennedy, when our new president and a Democratic Congress enacted sweeping civil rights legislation. But was the removal of the cloak of bigotry towards black people real or imagined?

Today, why is it difficult to find white people in the South whose allegiance is to the Democratic Party? From the time of the enactment of civil rights legislation in the 60's by the Democratic Party, until 2008, a Republican "Southern Strategy" has turned a previous hotbed of Democrats into a racist GOP bastion. However, the death knell of the Democratic Party in the South came in 2008, when the country had the audacity to elect a black Democratic president!

When the present Congress convened in 2012, there was only a few "Southern Democrats" in the U.S. House of Representatives out of total of one hundred five southern representatives. Democratic Congressmen in the South who survive represented urban areas where black people predominated. As for the U.S. Senate, Southern Democrats were practically extinct!

Below is an example of the racial intolerance remaining in today's south. One can also surmise the mindset and values of people by those they choose to honor. Mississippi had plans to issue a license plate honoring Confederate General Nathan Bedford Forrest, who not only commanded the massacre of black union soldiers at fort Pillow, Tennessee in 1864, but later formed and became the "Grand Wizard" of the Ku Klux Klan!

Racism in the south does have it limits, particularly when it comes to college football. Throughout the south in the fall, stadiums are filled to capacity with zealots screaming for victory by the home football team. Were there enough seats available, these stadiums would be filled ten times over. Ironically, although most of the fans are white, most of the players for college teams in today's desegregated south consist of black players! It seems that even white Southerners, who for most of the week are consumed by racism, become color-blind during the games. What a shame that this retreat from racism exists only on game day!

In today's difficult times, it is not surprising that many Americans look for someone or some group to blame for their lot in life, a scapegoat. Hispanics are a current "Boogyman"! Seven states with Republican Governors and legislatures, primarily in the south, are in the process of enacting legislation, similar to that previously enacted in Arizona,

Arizona's recent laws, which are of questionable constitutionality, allow law enforcement personnel to stop, detain and possibly arrest anyone that they "reasonably suspect" are in the country illegally. Of course, anyone who is "lily-white" will not be stopped and harassed. Hopefully, after this issue winds its way through lower courts and finally must be ruled on by the U.S. Supreme Court, even that ultra conservative court will not uphold such blatant racism. A high-ranking Arizona official joined in the attack on Hispanics by initiating legislation banning "Mexican-American" studies from being taught in Arizona schools.

Georgia and Alabama have also passed legislation attacking "illegal immigrants", the code word for Hispanics. Alabama has gone even further than Arizona, denying those deemed illegal the right to attend public schools. It is also illegal in Alabama for a citizen to give an undocumented person a ride in their automobile. One Republican lawmaker in Alabama even suggested that the solution to illegal immigrants was to "empty the clip" on those deemed illegal. Of course, the purpose of these laws is to encourage Hispanics to leave the state. In fact, many Hispanics have indeed gone "underground" or left the state. Ironically, Both Georgia and Alabama are suffering from this "exodus" of cheap labor. Now, on many farms in these states, crops are rotting on the vine for the lack of anyone willing to engage in this hard work. Those that do work in the fields demand higher wages than the previous "cheap labor". This results in higher prices to the consumer.

Many Americans who resent the presence of these "foreigners" suggest that they should all be deported to the country from whence they came. Although in 2010, a record number of illegal immigrants were deported, it is estimated that in excess of ten million illegal immigrants still presently reside in America. However, if all of these millions were to be deported, the cost to each man, woman and child legally residing in America would approach a thousand dollars each. Would it not be more reasonable for our government to allow all illegal immigrants who have been in America for a long time, have meaningful employment and have otherwise led model lives be given the opportunity to seek citizenship?

Another sad period in our history came shortly after the abhorrent sneak attack upon Pearl Harbor by the Japanese. Both our citizens and our government were both irate and irrational, resulting in unjustified retribution upon American citizens of Japanese descent who were confined for the duration of World War II in the squalor of internment camps. There only crime was that they were of a different race than "white" Americans. During the years that they suffered this humiliation, although America was at war with both Italy and Germany, Americans of Italian and German descent walked freely among us.

After "9-11", the same scenario is playing out again today, as loyal Americans of Islamic faith are castigated and denigrated by self-serving politicians hoping to capitalize upon the irrational fears and prejudices of otherwise decent people. Unfortunately, the public is "buying into" this despicable hatred.

Examples of Americans' intolerance toward those of the Muslim faith abound. Even Muslims who have lived in our country for many years and are model citizens find themselves the subject of irrational hate. Throughout America, protests are sure to follow when peaceful Muslims propose to build a house of worship. Also, in a county in Tennessee near Nashville, a local sheriff has hired an anti-Muslim fanatic to "indoctrinate" local police personnel in the "nuances" of the Muslim faith!

When, if ever, will our citizens become more tolerant of those of different religions, or races and learn to live in peace and harmony with everyone? Even during the very darkest days of World War II, President Franklin Roosevelt uttered words of wisdom that we should live by today;

"There is nothing to fear but fear itself"

CHAPTER 9

Education

A PRIMARY REASON for America's greatness is our long-standing emphasis on universal public education for all of our citizens. However, recent trends in educating our young people are alarming. States throughout the country are drastically decreasing the financial resources provided public schools. A quality public education is necessary is essential for an informed and intelligent workforce. In addition, programs initiated in a great number of states fund private education for the elite in our society at the expense of the masses who are less fortunate. Also, America continues to cling to an outdated "one size fits all" approach to education.

One reason that America is falling behind the rest of the world in educating our citizens is a failure by both our leaders and the average citizen to realize the importance of educating our children in order to compete in an increasingly complex and competitive world. In Asia, India and other developing countries, both the governments and parents put a premium on educating their young and keeping children's "nose to the grindstone"!

In contrast, although in previous generations of Americans teachers were revered and held in high esteem, this is no longer the case. In the past, when students were admonished at school for unruly or unsatisfactory behavior, the children were in even more trouble at home. Support for teachers was at a high level. Today, parents are prone to take their children's side of any dispute and often confront the beleaguered and frustrated teacher on their children's behalf. This lessens the respect for teachers by parents, children and society as a whole. This often results in excellent but frustrated teachers to seek other types of employment.

One recent development in our country is an attempt, often successful, to abolish tenure for teachers. Republicans lead the charge in this attempt. Thus teachers in states controlled by Republicans have little, if any, job security. They can be dismissed for spurious reasons, without cause, and replaced by unqualified political hacks beholden to the powers that be. Thus, even more competent and dedicated teachers either leave the profession, move to states where the emphasis is on quality education rather than political cronyism or seek employment in private schools.

In addition to the loss of qualified and dedicated teachers, many states are cutting hundreds of millions of dollars from their budgets for public schools. This results in a disturbing trend in many school systems to go to a 4-day school week, reducing by 20 percent the time public school students spend obtaining essential knowledge and skills. Also, many school systems are seriously reducing both teachers and ancillary staff, resulting in grossly over-sized classrooms and diminished support services.

Especially hard-hit by the lack of funds are kindergarten and pre-kindergarten classes, which may be seriously reduced or eliminated altogether. Education for the vey young is essential, especially for children mired in poverty with little, if any, learning experiences at home, if all of our citizens are to have a decent chance to compete in the workplace and in society as a whole. Of course, the wealthy among us have the financial wherewithal to send their children to private schools and, eventually, to prestigious colleges and universities. Accordingly, the financial elite, and the Republicans they help keep in office, have no concern how the "other half" lives and care not "one wit" what happens to the millions of less fortunate who predominate in our society!

In response to the continuing deterioration of our nation's public schools, alternative methods of educating children of the lower middle class and the impoverished have come to the forefront. Examples are Charter Schools, Magnet Schools and the issuance of educational "vouchers" to specified children. Theoretically, these programs enhance the chances of children of the "lower classes" to obtain a decent education.

The attempt to level the educational playing field by adopting any of the three above programs is but an illusion and "cruel joke" upon those attempting to utilize them. These programs actually help the favored few at the expense of those not fortunate enough to participate. Assignments to Charter and Magnet Schools are often based on the luck of the draw, with some sort of lottery used to determine the "lucky" winners. What about the children who are not chosen? Their fate is to be required to attend deteriorating public schools, often in the inner city, with little chance of ever competing with the "lucky few" for employment or in society.

As for states that have a "voucher system" to allow some students to attend schools much superior to public schools, only a very small percentage of students actually have a chance of being selected. Many of these voucher systems are created solely to allow Christian students to attend religious schools. This is particularly true in states controlled by Republicans, since religious zealots are usually the base of their political support. Since these vouchers come from taxpayer funds, even less state financial assistance is available to the public schools attended by the less fortunate in our society.

One particularly despicable misuse of funds in our educational system finds those intended to help the most vulnerable children in our society, the mentally and physically handicapped, are not always used for that purpose. Although the federal government provides funds to help fund "Special Ed" classes, political operatives, usually Republicans, convince uneducated and uninformed parents that their children would be better off in less costly alternative programs, which can be best described as "Fly-By-Night" programs of little value.

In the typical classroom in public schools, there is a significant difference in the intelligence and learning potential of the students. High achievers, average students and those that, through no fault of their own, must struggle to learn the assigned material are "lumped together" in the same classroom. By necessity, teachers are forced to spend a great deal of time on the "slow learners" to help them keep their heads above water. This leaves other students, particularly the intelligent and intellectually curious, bored, with a tendency to lose interest in the material altogether. Thus, a great many in the class fail to achieve their intellectual potential.

A more beneficial approach for all students would be to initiate a "Three-Tier" system. Classrooms should be divided into three distinct groups: (1) high achievers and the intellectually curious (2) average students and (3) students requiring special attention to learn the required material. Using this system, the educational needs of all can be achieved. Social considerations must have no part in dividing the class into distinct groups. Intelligence, aptitude and a desire for knowledge should be the sole determining criteria.

The "No Child Left Behind" program, dreamed up many years ago when Republicans controlled the federal government, has proved to be a disaster! Although the legislation had good intentions, it has resulted in the nation's teachers "teaching to the test", attempting to enable students to do well on required achievement tests, rather than developing innovative and proactive thinking in students. Creative thinking was stifled to such an extent that students were almost never encouraged to "think out of the box". Even by "teaching to the test", teachers were unable to enable students to meet federal achievement standards. In addition, ACT test results have plummeted at an alarming rate.

In addition to a decline in test scores and the failure to provide students with stimulating and challenging material, unfortunately in many instances, our nation's classrooms have been bombarded with political and religious meddling. At the behest of Republican naysayers, books which would have provided students with inquisitive and controversial subject matter to help develop young minds, have been banned by narrow minded school officials throughout the land! In Missouri, an award winning book, which had gotten rave reviews from book critics, was banned because it violated "community standards". In Texas, probably the most reactionary state in the union, the Texas Board of Education passed a resolution that forbade references to "Islam" in textbooks. Since there are almost two billions members of the Islamic faith on Earth, and a only small minority of that faith threaten America, are Texans supposed to bury their heads in the sand and pretend that they do not exist?

One harmful concept prominent throughout our country is that the only way an American can achieve success and live the "American Dream" is to obtain a college education and perhaps even further advanced education. This concept is harmful in two respects. First, it should be obvious that not every child possesses either sufficient native intelligence and intellectual curiosity or the financial wherewithal to see a college degree as a sensible goal. Secondly, Even if utopia was possible and every American student obtained a college degree, the supply of jobs where a college education is required, or even helpful, is limited. Millions of young people would be much better off concentrating on obtaining technical or work skills not requiring a college education. Skilled workers are hard to find. Further, many skilled workers receive much more financial remuneration than marginal college graduates who often end up in unsatisfactory non-challenging jobs.

Since traditional reputable colleges and universities of higher learning cannot possibly admit the hordes of applicants, an insidious industry to "rip-off" the unsuspecting young person wishing to better their lot in life has developed. The culprit: the "For-Profit" educational institution. Although there are a few exceptions, most of these "For-Profits" are only out to make a "fast buck". Not surprisingly, these entities are much more expensive that traditional institutions of higher learning. Also, graduation rates are very low. The worst aspect of these "scams" is that employers, aware that there is no short-cut to learning, are well aware of the inferior training of these "graduates" and are not likely to hire graduates of these "diploma mills"! The degrees obtained are almost worthless!

Many young people today who, having obtained a college degree or have been the victim of the "For-Profit" scams, and expected a high paying job and the "good life" now find themselves disillusioned. Today, many college graduates either, due to a dearth of available jobs, find themselves forced to work in jobs far below their previous expectations. Many are also unable to find work of any kind! Even worse, a large percentage of these graduates of traditional colleges and of course, the victims of "For Profits", find themselves buried themselves under a mountain of debt from student loans.

Student loans have become to many of the young the "Elephant in the Room"! Student loans, for educational pursuits in both traditional colleges and the "ballooning for Profit" schools are either obtained from the federal government or even worse, from disreputable people that charge enormous interest rates. Student loans are a tremendous burden upon students, particularly when, upon graduation, they are able to obtain only low paying jobs or no jobs at all. Many are forced to default on the loans, injurious to their credit rating and prospects for future success. The true magnitude of the problem cannot be over emphasized! Amazingly, the total amount due for student loans amounts to trillions of dollars, exceeding the total credit card debt of all Americans!

With decent jobs hard to find, salaries stagnant, and having an avalanche of student debt, young people face a future far different from their parents. The life styles of this "lost Generation" will be impaired for many years. Marriages and the starting a family will most likely be delayed. Buying a home will not be possible in the foreseeable future. At present, the American Dream seems to be but an illusion of the past! But there is hope not only for young people but for all Americans if the reactionary politicians, mostly Republicans, who have brought us into this sorry state by passing legislation making the rich richer, the poor poorer and the middle class slowly fade away, are replaced by Democrats bent on restoring the American Dream for all Americans.

CHAPTER 10

Foreign Policy

SINCE THE DAYS of our founding fathers, missteps have occasionally been made in the administration of our foreign policy. However, until the last half of the twentieth century, most of our errors in dealing with other nations have been inconsequential in their effect on the fabric of our society. Our time-worn emphasis on the freedom of the individual has remained one of America's basic principles.

In the 1960's, this basic principle became subverted as far as the people of other countries were concerned. President Johnson, using the Bay of Tonkin incident as a pretext, inexplicably ordered an invasion of Vietnam in support of a ruthless dictator with no regard for how he mistreated his country's people. The excuse used for abandoning this fundamental principle was that if we did not stop the spread of "Communism", we would soon we fighting them "on our shores". Of course, after over ten years of bloody conflict and the demise of the dictator we supported, and with hundreds of thousands of American casualties, we ultimately suffered the humiliation of abandoning a lost cause. As for the victorious Vietnamese, they proved to be no threat to either America or any other country. They simply wanted the right to govern themselves without outside interference. One would have thought that the horrific experience in Vietnam would have taught our leaders an important lesson, that countries and their people simply wished to be left alone to govern themselves. Unfortunately, the lesson was lost on some future leaders!

Ever since Vietnam, America has further abandoned the precious ideal of freedom of the individual in order to "win friends", particularly in the Middle East. Often, dictators and tyrants in the Middle East, who ruled with an iron hand and grossly subjugated the basic human rights of their subjects, have received both the support and "friendship" of our leaders and billions in foreign aid. For decades, "cozying up" to these tyrants, despite being inconsistent with our nation's time-honored values, appeared to be in the "temporary" best interest of our country. But years later, abandoning our basic values proved to be a disaster.

A previous chapter revealed the financial ruin, which devastated America's economy, by the two unwarranted, irresponsible and almost endless wars in Iraq and Afghanistan. However, the real tragedy is the almost complete destruction of both of these countries and devastation of the lives of hordes of innocent people.

As a result of the war in Iraq, ten percent of the women in the country were war widows, living lives of utter desperation. The infrastructure of Iraq was almost completely obliterated. Perhaps feeling some sense of guilt, America eventually spent billions of dollars attempting to rebuild the infrastructure destroyed during the senseless war. Ultimately, many of the projects were completely abandoned! Finally, in 2011, President Obama had enough of the war first commenced almost ten years before by his predecessor, George W. Bush, and ordered all of the troops to withdraw from Iraq and "come home". The Iraqis did not say "thank you", but instead "good riddance"!

After ten years of war, costing America's taxpayers to pay "through the nose" and helping destroy America' economy, what was the state of the Iraq we left behind? In 20ll, having suffered hundreds of thousands of dead and wounded, including civilians, Iraq was totally devastated. As for the warring religious factions, nothing had changed. They continued the hatred and constant infighting that had been a part of their history since time immemorial. Ultimately, the "fragile" government we left behind has very little chance of surviving.

As for the war in Afghanistan which also was started by President George W. Bush in 2001 and, ten years later, has no end in sight. What have we accomplished? Afghanistan's president regularly "thumbs his nose" at any recommendations given by our leaders. Torture of detainees is routinely administered by the government. The cost of providing security is astronomical. Warlords still "rule the day" and have control of much of the financial aid provided by the American taxpayer. With friends like the Afghan government, "we don't need enemies"! President Obama, if fortunate enough to be re-elected, has promised that he will end the war in Afghanistan within a couple of years. Instead, he should just "bite the bullet" and bring the troops home "NOW"! Of course this would incur the wrath of Republicans in Congress, most of whom "have never met a war they didn't like"!

Beginning in the very recent past, the benefits of our policy of mollifying and "cozying up" to Mideast dictators, is beginning to unravel. Egypt is a good example of American foreign policy gone wrong. President Mubarak, had ruled Egypt with an iron fist, with little regard for his subjects, for thirty years. During those thirty years, Egypt received billions in aid from America to "prop up" his regime. President George W. Bush's Vice-President, Dick Cheney, even referred to President Mubarak as a "good friend" of the United States.

America's leaders got a "wake up call" concerning the policy of befriending and supporting despots, when in early 2011, engaged Egyptians, tired of president Mubarak's abuses drove him from office. This was just the beginning of the end for America's "friendly" Middle East tyrannical rulers, though the final result will not be played out for many years. As the vast communication system throughout the world spreads the word of one country's rebellion, citizens of other countries suffering similarly, are given the strength and courage to rise up against their leaders. Consequently, there exists throughout the entire Middle East an increasing confidence among the disadvantaged that better days lay ahead.

Realizing that they have "backed the wrong horse", our country's leaders are attempting to back-track and now give "lip service" to supporting the rebels who have overthrown or are attempting to overthrow America's former "friends". Countries that have been liberated or now are in the process of rebellion have a myriad of problems to face. It may take many years before these massive problems are at last remedied by new leaders and new stable governments emerge.

CHAPTER 11

Military

AMERICANS HAVE EXPRESSED gratitude for the valiant citizens who answered their country's call and served proudly in the military services. Especially noteworthy, are the millions who volunteered to defend our country after the infamous attack on Pearl Harbor. In World War II, military personnel served for the duration of the war, no matter how long the war lasted. They truly were the "Greatest Generation"! Unfortunately, today's American military is but a shadow of its former self. When did this steady downhill slide of our military begin?

In all of America's wars, up until and including the War in Vietnam, a universal draft provided our military forces with citizens from all walks of life, who generally served with a sense of comradeship. During the War in Vietnam, there was much dissent among draft age young people because the war was obviously completely unnecessary and contrary to the best interest of our country. However, although the war was divisive, because no "class" in our society was singled out to suffer the entire burden of the war, there was a resigned feeling of "shared sacrifice".

What Happened to the American Dream?

As for the War in Vietnam itself, I have a personal perspective. In the fall of 1965, I was attending the University of Tennessee, expecting to graduate in December of that year. Vietnam was farthest from my thoughts, seeming "light years" away. In September, I got a "wake up call", when I checked with my draft board and found that I was "first in line" to be drafted upon graduation. Had there not been a draft, there is no way that I would have volunteered to serve in such an unjust and evil war. However, realizing that military service was inevitable, I desperately applied to Naval Officer Candidate School (OCS)! I found that graduating seniors from other colleges and universities throughout the country, many of which were more prestigious than "UT", were in the "same boat". Even though with such ardent competition, I was fortunate enough to be accepted!

After successfully completing both OCS in Newport, Rhode Island, and further training as a Supply Officer at the Naval Supply Corps School in Athens, Georgia, my first permanent duty station was aboard the USS Frontier (AD-25), in Long Beach, California. Unfortunately, a great tour aboard the USS Frontier ended in May of 1968, at which time I had approximately one year remaining on my commitment to the Navy. Not surprisingly, the powers that be "shipped me off" to the U. S. Naval Support Activity in Danang, South Vietnam, where, after serving there a year, my military service came to an end!

In Vietnam, there were a few "gung ho" military personnel who had volunteered to serve in the war. Some were on their second or third tour. However, as might be expected, the vast majority consisted of "draftees" who had decided to grin and bare serving a year in Vietnam rather ran turn tail and run off to Canada as so many other young men had done.

After settling into my duties at the Supply Depot in Danang, to my surprise, many of the enlisted personnel of whom I was in charge, were highly educated, having degrees from colleges or universities. Another surprise was that the moral of the draftees was much better than I had anticipated. This could be attributed to the fact that, unlike present day soldiers, who serve tour after tour, everyone knew that if they could survive one year in the "Nam", they would never have to return. I must admit that upon my first arriving in Vietnam, it was somewhat disconcerting to be among so many "short timers", who were counting the days until they returned home. Every single military person in Vietnam, both officers and enlisted men, knew exactly how many days they had remaining in the war zone before they could return home and restart their lives. Unfortunately, when we returned home from Vietnam, we were often spit on, cursed and treated like we had betrayed our country.

At last, after years of sacrifice by our soldiers, the war finally ended in a humiliating defeat. Americans faced much angst having to deal with experiencing the hundreds of thousands of casualties for such a "lost cause". I would be remiss if I did not also comment on the fate of the thousands of Vietnamese who worked alongside and trusted American forces in Vietnam. No doubt, for supporting the Americans, many were either killed or forced to work in intolerable labor camps for the rest of their lives. I try my best to not think of what happened to the Vietnamese friends that I made. Their fate haunts me to this day!

During the latter stages of the War in Vietnam, our government had to deal with the intensive protests by our citizens over both the draft and the war. To mollify the rich and middle class, our leaders reached the unfortunate decision to establish an "all volunteer military". The fallacy of this decision was not readily apparent. After the War in Vietnam ended, our country was very fortunate that for decades there was no significant military ventures occurring throughout the world that would have required massive numbers of troops to be deployed. However, with the election of George W. Bush as president in 2000, that all changed! After "9-11" inexplicably, President took it upon himself to initiate two disastrous wars. The War in Iraq lasted almost ten years. There is no assurance that the fragile Iraqi government left behind will not eventually be overthrown. The War in Afghanistan is now in its eleventh year, with no end in sight. President Obama should just "declare victory" And bring the troops home now! As or the results of decision to go to an all volunteer military, our once proud fighting machine began to "come unglued"!

What those that instigated the volunteer military failed to understand was that, without the threat of a draft, educated children of the middle class would have no incentive to join the military, since much better options were available to them. Some of the poorest among us, many having only minimal skills, were willing to serve and perhaps face death because they had few if any other options. Thus, it became very difficult for the military to meet the required quotas of new recruits, without being forced to accept some who had major issues. Many who that in past wars would have found unacceptable became members of our military. In addition, because of the difficulty in finding recruits who met even the diminished standards, the military became greatly understaffed. By necessity, those that did serve were often required to serve multiple tours in either Iraq or Afghanistan, with little time off between tours, greatly increasing their chances of either being killed or seriously injured.

Because of the nature of the wars in Iraq and Afghanistan, with the enemy's massive use of booby-traps and high-tech percussion bombs, the number of injured soldiers was much greater than might have been expected. Brain injuries to soldiers were a major problem. Many Veterans' hospital were not equipped to handle such a large number of casualties. Also,

Due to the deplorable conditions in both war zones and the fact that many military personnel served multiple tours, it is not surprising that many of the combatants turned to the use of "meth", marijuana and cocaine. Criminal activity also increased accordingly. Even worse, there was also a troubling spike in the number of troops committing suicide!

What could veterans of these two wars expect if they survived, were discharged from service, and returned home to America? Many surprisingly found that their extensive military training did not necessarily mesh with the needs of American employers. Thus, the unemployment rate of veterans of Iraq and Afghanistan exceeds that of veterans of America's previous wars. Even worse, a very large percentage of those unable to find employment, find themselves living alone, homeless without family ties.

Since the sons and daughters of the rich and middle class do not share the burden of the mostly poor military veterans, it is not surprising that their elected representatives in the government do not find the plight of the veterans worthy of concern. However, it should always be remembered that the way a country treats those who have served honorably to protect their country, is a measure of the humanity of that country and its citizens!

CHAPTER 12

Crime

THE AMERICAN DREAM is personified in our glorious National Anthem, which depicts our country as the "home of the free". This optimistic outlook is very valid for most of our countrymen, unless they happen to be poor or are a member of a minority. In America, over two million citizens are now behind bars. Even though our country represents only 5 percent of the world's population, we have 25 percent of those incarcerated throughout the world. Since 1980, the number of imprisoned Americans has swollen from five hundred thousand in 1980 to a greatly in excess of two million today. This represents an extreme tax burden on our country. The cost of housing prisoners seriously undermines our ability to provide essential educational and social services to our citizens.

As stated above, courthouses, jails and prisons overflow with the poor and minorities who usually are punished much more severely than rich and Middle Class whites for similar offenses. Almost half of those serving time are incarcerated for non-violent offenses for which alternative punishments, such as house arrest with appropriate monitoring devices, would appear much more reasonable and less costly. Also, costs associated with the incarceration of many aging inmates who are no longer a threat to society further burden prison systems.

One aspect of American life contributing greatly to excessive violence here is the "wild west mentality" and an obsession with guns of many of our citizens. The number of murders in America is astronomical. In contrast, in Canada where the number of guns per capita mirrors that of the United States, the number of murders committed by Canadians is extremely low. Here, controls over the sale and distribution of firearms are practically non-existent. Guns are readily available, even to the mentally disturbed, to anyone desirous of such an instrument of destruction. Gun shows, exhibiting every kind of firearm imaginable, even those deemed illegal, are prevalent throughout the country. Some states go so far as legalizing and encouraging the possession of guns on college campuses. Why is it surprising that, a few years ago, a mentally deranged man at Virginia Tech University killed 32 people and wounded 25 more and, more recently, another psychopath murdered several people and seriously wounded a Congresswomen from Arizona?

There is a dichotomy in America's legal system that is very hard to comprehend, the different legal approach to two substances, alcohol and marijuana. First, take the case of marijuana. Although a recent poll indicated that a majority of Americans favor legalizing the possession of a small amount of marijuana, most police forces are obsessed with catching "criminals" using that substance. Perhaps it is a lot easier (and safer) to go after the non-violent users of marijuana than dangerous hardened criminals who wreck havoc upon the innocent in our society. Further, the countless citizens serving time for the casual use of marijuana are responsible for filling prisons to the brim, allowing perpetrators of serious crimes to get early releases. The "War on Drugs", of which Republicans are the most ardent advocates, is an utter failure because it focuses primarily on apprehending casual users of marijuana, who are no threat to society, rather than tackling the many more serious criminals who prey upon our innocent citizens. Why is marijuana use so prevalent, especially among America's young? As can be proven in the case of alcohol, anytime a substance is deemed illegal, human nature kicks in and deems the banned substance more attractive than if its use was legal.

In the roaring 20's, self-righteous politicians managed to enact "Prohibition" banning the sale and consumption of alcohol. The result was what one might expect. First, many Americans who, before prohibition, had no inclination or interest in consuming alcohol, flaunted the law in every conceivable manner just to take a "drink". Secondly, taking advantage of the ban on alcohol, criminals of every sort turned to selling the illegal substance to a desperate public. As a result, not only did hardened criminals become rich, but all manner of crime, including murder, was rampant throughout America. Thanks to President Franklin Roosevelt, after years of turmoil, prohibition was finally recognized as an utter failure and alcohol once again became legally available to the public.

Ironically, compared to casual users of illegal marijuana, the legal consumption of alcohol is a bane upon society. Drivers who over-imbibe are responsible for countless deaths on our highways. Countless offenders, with innumerable arrests for driving under the influence, get a slap on the wrist and are soon back on the streets to continue their carnage! When will we finally "get it" and base the length of incarceration on whose behavior is most detrimental to society?

As to the fairness of the legal system, the financial condition and/or the race of an offender, unfortunately, are often paramount in determining whether justice is truly served. The poor and minorities, often ignorant of their rights and without financial wherewithal, have a much greater chance than of being convicted of a crime irrespective of their guilt or innocence. They also usually serve more time incarcerated than those with financial means for similar offenses. This inequity is especially true where the death penalty is imposed. Have you ever heard of a wealthy or Middle Class white citizen actually being executed? Some states are more notorious than others for their eagerness to "hang um high"! You certainly don't want to be black or indigent in Texas!

As for getting a fair trial, good luck if you are indigent in some states. As for legal representation for the accused, 13 of the 15 states with the largest prison populations, a fee is charged in order to have access to a public defender. In some states, application fees for access to an attorney often resulted in indigent Americans accused of a crime from learning of their rights under the U.S. Constitution. Throughout America, innocent people from the bottom of society have a much greater chance of being found guilty! It pays to be born rich!

Republicans, who usually come from middle or upper class families and are "lily-white", cannot relate to and have no sympathy for the desperate plight of minorities and poor white people relegated to the very bottom of society. Most Republicans honestly believe that they deserve their elevated status, even though often they were born into wealth and have done absolutely nothing to deserve their "good fortune". Most assume that their wealth and birthright justifies their prominent place in both politics and society.

CHAPTER 13

2012 Election

THIS BOOK IS going to press in early March 2012. At this time, the Republican nominee for president has yet to be determined. I will not speculate as to who will be the eventual Republican presidential candidate in 2012 or to the outcome of the general election in November. However, I do have observations with regard to the current campaign to determine the Republican nominee.

The Republican Party once claimed to be the party of "compassionate conservatism". This moderate tone appealed to many of our citizens, including many who tended to be independent when casting their vote. However, in the quest to determine the Republican nominee for president in 2012, the many debates by Republicans seeking the nomination revealed an extremist agenda by the candidates!

Consistent with the extreme rhetoric by the Republican candidates, a radical element attending the Republican debates have not only been mean-spirited but have expressed outright contempt for many Americans suffering the most during the current recession. They "booed and ridiculed" a soldier who had valiantly served his country, simply because that soldier was "gay". They also cheered loudly the death of a poor person who could not afford life-saving health care. In addition, this "mob" expressed ridicule upon those in our society forced to depend upon food stamps.

One reason that the Republican Party has drifted so far to the extreme right is their fear of the "mindless" members of the Tea Party. This fear is well founded! Due to the desperation of a great many Americans suffering from the current severe recession, the Tea Party made significant gains in the U.S. House of Representatives in the 2010 mid-term elections. Unfortunately for Republicans, even very conservative Republican members of the House were victims of the "purge". Emboldened by their success in 2010, the Tea Party has expanded its horizons. Their goal in the 2012 elections is to unseat even more very conservative Republicans in Congress and replace them with Tea Party faithful. Because the Republican Party feared loosing its grip on its power, they forged an "unholy alliance" with the Tea Party.

As a consequence of the above alliance, all progressive legislation proposed by President Obama or Democrats in the Democrat controlled U.S. Senate has been "dead on arrival" when it reached the House. However, this "war" cuts both ways. Any radical legislation proposed by the House faces a certain death in the Senate or, in the unlikely event of Senate passage, a certain veto by President Obama! Consequently, for the remainder of 2012, and perhaps even longer depending on the result of the Congressional and presidential elections in November, our government is completely paralyzed, unable to address even the most basic needs of our citizens!

Although through the years our elections have become increasingly costly, the fairly recent U.S. Supreme Court decision allowing the wealthy and corporate America to donate unlimited funds to influence elections has opened the floodgates to the possible "buying" of elections! "Super-PACs" are now receiving vast sums for both political parties and political candidates. Since millionaires and billionaires and Corporate CEO's greatly benefit when the government is in Republican hands, it is not surprising that Republican friendly "PACs" rake in far more than those supporting Democratic candidates.

During the 2012 Republican primaries to determine President Obama's November opponent, the greatest Republican benefactor of the hundreds of millions made available by these PACs was Mitt Romney. Attacks against his Republican opponents proliferate on television. It remains to be seen whether Mr. Romney will obtain the Republican nomination for president, however, if he does it will be money that tells the difference.

Just what is the Republican plan on unseating President Obama? Essentially the plan is to convince middle class Americans that the country will benefit by greatly reducing the tax rate of millionaires and billionaires. Hidden from the average American is that such a vast reduction in taxes would by necessity result in a reduction in the "safety net" provided both the middle class and our poor citizens. Targeted by Republicans for drastic cuts or elimination are Social Security, Medicare, Medicaid, food stamps and any other program that Republicans claim benefit only the "lazy" among us!

What "devilment" are Republicans up to in states where they control the state governments, particularly in the South? Hoping to expand upon their majority in the House of Representatives they obtained as a result of the 2010 mid-term elections, Republicans are using the time-old technique of "gerrymandering" to minimize the political power of black people. They dilute the power of the black vote by "corralling" them in almost completely black Congressional districts, so that they would have no influence in swing or crossover districts.

On the federal level, President Obama continues to initiate proposals that would address the vast problems our country now faces. However, with extremist Republicans and their Tea Party cohorts firmly in control of the House, everything he proposes is "dead on arrival". To no avail, he has called for increases in the tax rate for the wealthiest Americans in order to address the out-of-control budget deficit. Any time a proposal is made by Democrats to make the Rich pay their fair share, the Republicans always claim "class warfare". In truth, class warfare already exists in America, with the "upper class" living the "life of Riley", while average middle class and poor Americans attempt to just survive!

The 2012 Congressional and presidential elections will be a defining time in America, determining the direction our country will take. Basically, American voters have three alternatives. The first alternative is completely unacceptable, leaving our country divided between progressive Democrats and reactionary Republicans, with constant bickering and hopeless gridlock, while our country's massive problems remain unaddressed.

The second alternative is even worse, turning the government over completely to Republicans and their Tea Party cohorts, resulting in the rich getting richer, the poor getting poorer and the middle class disappearing. The only hope for our country to find rational solutions to our problems is to return state governments to Democratic rule, re-elect President Obama, continue the Democratic majority in the U.S. Senate and throw the Republican and Tea Party extremists out of the U.S. House of Representatives!

CPSIA information can be obtained at www.ICGtesting.com
Printed in the USA
BVOW04s2153280414

351993BV00001B/33/P